IT'S TIME TO EAT MUNG BEANS

It's Time to Eat
MUNG BEANS

Walter the Educator

Silent King Books
A WhichHead Entertainment Imprint

Copyright © 2025 by Walter the Educator

All rights reserved. No part of this book may be reproduced in any manner whatsoever without written per- mission except in the case of brief quotations embodied in critical articles and reviews.

First Printing, 2024

Disclaimer

This book is a literary work; the story is not about specific persons, locations, situations, and/or circumstances unless mentioned in a historical context. Any resemblance to real persons, locations, situations, and/or circumstances is coincidental. This book is for entertainment and informational purposes only. The author and publisher offer this information without warranties expressed or implied. No matter the grounds, neither the author nor the publisher will be accountable for any losses, injuries, or other damages caused by the reader's use of this book. The use of this book acknowledges an understanding and acceptance of this disclaimer.

It's Time to Eat MUNG BEANS is a collectible early learning book by Walter the Educator suitable for all ages belonging to Walter the Educator's Time to Eat Book Series. Collect more books at WaltertheEducator.com

USE THE EXTRA SPACE TO TAKE NOTES AND DOCUMENT YOUR MEMORIES

MUNG BEANS

It's time to eat, hooray, hooray!

It's Time to Eat

Mung Beans

Mung beans make a yummy day.

So small and round, so green and bright,

A little bean that's just so right!

They start off tiny, smooth, and green,

But cook them up, and what a scene!

They turn so soft, they taste just great,

A healthy snack right on your plate!

Mung beans grow where the sun shines bright,

In fields of green, a lovely sight!

Farmers pick them, clean, and pack,

Then send them out for every snack!

You can eat them in a stew,

In a soup or salad too!

Mash them, sprout them, cook them slow,

So many ways to make them go!

It's Time to Eat

Mung Beans

Mung beans help you jump and run,

They give you strength for lots of fun!

They help you learn and help you grow,

They're super good, just so you know!

Some like them sweet, some like them plain,

Some mix them up with rice and grain.

In bowls or wraps, in soups or more,

Mung beans are a treat for sure!

Tiny sprouts can start to grow,

Watch them wiggle, watch them show!

Crunchy, fresh, so fun to eat,

A sprouty snack can't be beat!

Try one bite, just give it a go,

You might just love it, you never know!

A spoon, a fork, or with your hand,

It's Time to Eat

Mung Beans

Eating mung beans is so grand!

Healthy, tasty, warm or cool,

Mung beans are a super fuel!

So grab a bowl and take a seat,

It's time to eat, what a treat!

Munch, munch, hooray, hooray!

Mung beans make a happy day.

A little bean with power inside,

It's Time to Eat

Mung Beans

Let's eat them up with joy and pride!

ABOUT THE CREATOR

Walter the Educator is one of the pseudonyms for Walter Anderson. Formally educated in Chemistry, Business, and Education, he is an educator, an author, a diverse entrepreneur, and he is the son of a disabled war veteran. "Walter the Educator" shares his time between educating and creating. He holds interests and owns several creative projects that entertain, enlighten, enhance, and educate, hoping to inspire and motivate you. Follow, find new works, and stay up to date with Walter the Educator™

at WaltertheEducator.com

www.ingramcontent.com/pod-product-compliance
Lightning Source LLC
LaVergne TN
LVHW052013060526
838201LV00059B/4011